Listening to the Silence

The Seasons of Grief

Compiled by Jim Blommer.

Scripture quotations herein are from the *New Revised Standard Version Bible, Catholic Edition*, copyright ©2004, 1993 by the Division of Christian Education of the National Council of the Churches of Christ in the United States of America and are used by permission. All rights reserved by O.S.B.

CREDITS

Brother Placid Stuckenschneider, OSB

Dozens of book jackets and covers and hundreds of illustrations in bulletins and books published by The Liturgical Press since 1965 have featured the art of Brother Placid Stuckenschneider, OSB, a monk of St. John's Abbey. An artist who excels in various media from cartooning to pen and wash drawings, from welded metal to wood sculpture, to a ceramic mural. Brother Placid's talents are also widely known apart from book publishing. In post World War II Japan, he drew cartoons for the U.S. Army's *Pacific Stars and Stripes*. His full-color line drawings appeared regularly in the *St. Cloud Visitor* and occasionally in other diocesan papers, such as Milwaukee's *The Catholic Herald-Citizen*. Since Vatican Council II, over thirty parishes in Minnesota and the Dakotas have commissioned Brother Placid, a liturgical design consultant, to direct the renovation of church naves and sanctuaries. Brother Placid was on the team of five stained glass craftsmen who assembled the huge 430 hexagon window designed by Bronislaw Bak for the Abbey Church at St. John's University, Collegeville, Minnesota, in 1960. An ongoing project, over the years, has been to provide some ten art pieces, dedicated to various Saints, for private altars in various media, ceramic, welding and carving. Brother Placid has studied art at the Layton Art School, Milwaukee; the University of Notre Dame; the Blackhawk Mountain School of Art in Colorado; the Sagrada Art Studio, Albuquerque; and the Instituto Allende, San Miguel de Allende, Guanajuato, Mexico.

Special thanks to

- Brother Placid Stuckenschneider, OSB, for his expertise in photography.
- Mr. Jack Schneider for choosing appropriate Scripture verses.
- To writers, Fr. Paul Marx, OSB, Mr. Jim Blommer, Fr. Al Stangl, Sr. Georganne Burr, OSB, Fr. Robert Fox, and Diane M. Bösl. (Feel free to write to any of the writers at P.O. Box 475, Waite Park, MN 56387-0475)
- To Park Press personnel including Kelly Renken, Frank Freund, Bob Briggs (Prepress); Wayne Halena, Rick Gothier, Bruce Kitowski (Press); Rich Olson and Bindery Crew.

Dedicated to Dorothy with love.

DOROTHY WAS A MARVELOUS WIFE, a great mother to her children and a patient worker with her husband. I always found her to be very kind, generous and understanding. At the end of her life, which came slowly in her final days and weeks, I saw a wonderful woman who courageously faced death without a single complaint.

Dorothy clung to her faith and practiced it to the end with true Christian resignation to her forthcoming holy death after receiving all the sacraments such as the Church had for her and which helped in consoling her children.

While every death is a tragedy, those who live a beautifully Christian life find the gateway to Heaven which we read of in the Scriptures, "Eye has not seen, nor ear heard, what God has prepared for those who love Him." And for one

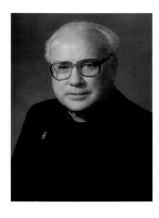

who lived as a holy wife and devoted mother, the Lord of Life surely has very special blessings and joys in the days that never end in Heaven.

It is for us to pray for her holy soul, to be edified by the way she lived her beautiful Christian life and prepared for a holy death and entrance into Heaven. For all this, Dorothy's life and resignation to the will of God is an example of the truly good life as wife and mother that she led, such as one can only wish for all those who are left behind. We should be edified by her good and saintly Christian life and her holy and peaceful death.

May all of us who knew her and admired her keep her always in our prayers and memories, knowing full well that in living a Christian life we shall see her again and be with her for all eternity. Let us remember her as a holy example of how to live a fully Christian life, no matter what the crosses and pains and sufferings that the Lord allows and allots.

—Fr. Paul Marx, OSB

TABLE OF CONTENTS

 Fr. Paul Marx, OSB
Dedication, page 4

 Sr. Georganne Burr, OSB, page 23

 Jim Blommer,
Foreword, page 8

 Fr. Robert J. Fox, page 35

 Fr. Al Stangl, page 9

 Diane M. Bösl, M.S., L.P., L.I.C.S.W.
page 49

 All Photography, Br. Placid Stuckenschneider, OSB

PICTURE LOCATIONS

p 11: Clouds of Love

p 12: Landscape: Christ in the Desert Monastery, New Mexico

p 13: Church at sunset: Spring Hill, Minnesota

p 14: Horses grazing: Lincoln, Montana

p 15: Native American teepees: Seeley Lake, Montana

p 16: Sunset over mountain: Deming, New Mexico

p 17: River rapids: Blackfoot River, Montana

p 18: Lake with mountains: Glacier National Park, Montana

p 19: Sunset: Flensburg, Minnesota

p 20: Unidentified sunset

p 21: Corn crib: near Sauk Centre, Minnesota

p 22: Colorado: near Aspen

p 25: Shocked oats: near Sauk Centre, Minnesota

p 26: Old fashioned harvest: south of Avon, Minnesota

p 27: St. John's woods

p 28: Deepwoods: St. John's woods

p 29: Mountainview: Alaska

p 30: Daffodils: Minnesota

p 31: Lady wth Flowers: Blackhawk, Colorado

p 32: Cactus: Colorado

p 33: Yellow flowers

p 34: Apparition Hill, Medjugorje

p 39: Body and Blood of Christ

p 40: Origins of St. John's

p 41: U.S. Bishops meeting: St. John's Abbey, Minnesota

p 42: Brother Hubert, St. John's Abbey, Minnesota

p 43: Sunset: North Santa Fe, New Mexico

p 44: Lake Morraine, Canada

p 45: Leaves in the woods

p 46: Fall Woods: St. John's woods

p 47: Mountain view with flowers: Banff, Alberta, Canada

p 48: Sunset: near Island Lake, Minnesota

p 51: Curious child: St. John's Abbey, Minnesota

p 52: Spiderweb: Minnesota

p 53: Waterfall: western Canada

p 54: Collapsing sheep barn: Colorado

p 55: St. Peter's, Rome

p 56: Fountain: St. Peter's, Rome

p 57: Fisherman: Kenai Peninsula, Alaska

p 58: Trout stream: Colorado

p 59: Mountain goat: Colorado

p 60: Holsteins: in farm country

p 61: Tree: Christ in the Desert Monastery, New Mexico

p 62: Boat dock at sunset: Swenson Lake, Minnesota

p 63: Sunset: Elrosa, Minnesota

"**G**RIEF" WAS A WORD with little meaning for me before last fall. Then it hit me like a cold glass of water. The love of my life, the mother of my children, my constant companion and best friend, died of cancer. What a hollow feeling her loss left in me. Only those who have lost a loved one can truly understand the hurt. I have always said that marriage binds a couple like two strings of twine that, when united, start to interweave as their lives progress. Year after year, a rope keeps growing and gaining strength. But when one of the partners dies, the rope becomes frazzled at the end and is never the same. Its strength is gone.

Where does one go from here? How does one manage to carry on? There is no ready-made, simple answer to fit every situation. Everyone must find his own way. Everyone must grieve in his own heart and struggle to find compensation and hope. I believe my wife is in a better place, a place where we will be united again some day.

Family and friends are truly one's best hope in helping during the grieving process. My daughters are my salvation. Their love keeps me going. It took me a while to realize that they were also grieving and we could share our loss. Words from me or words from them could comfort the other. We are now at the stage where we can recall all the good times we have shared together. We seemed to unite as a family, even confessing how angry we were at God for taking Dorothy's life. They say that time will heal the wound. Maybe. But the deep love will never fade. Little cherished moments will always be there, awaiting recall when one least expects them, causing one to smile in delight, even during stressful times, remembering how Dorothy had handled it, or expressed herself. My hope is that this book will help you on your journey.

—Jim Blommer

Blessed are they who mourn,
For they will be comforted.

T HESE WORDS OF JESUS at the Sermon of the Mount are a fitting introduction to this reflective book on grief and mourning. Jesus Himself experienced losses in His life. Although there is no Biblical reference to Joseph's death, I'm sure his death took place during Jesus' time at Nazareth. The death of a parent is a major loss, one of the four major deaths we all need to deal with in life. The others are death of a spouse, a child and our own death. Jesus also had the death of his close friend, Lazarus. St. John tells us of the event and how Jesus was perturbed and also wept. There are other times in Scripture when Jesus wept. There were other losses not connected with death. One example is a church in Jerusalem named "Dominus Flevit" ("The Lord Wept"). He wept over the City of Jerusalem, as they did not listen to His message. Very tenderly He used the image of a mother hen gathering her chicks around her; so did Christ try to gather around Him the people of Israel. Instead, they scattered and tried to kill Him. He wept out of sadness and rejection. I'm sure in the Garden of Olives He also wept as He sweat blood.

His followers also experienced their grief in losses and they too mourned. Mary wept as Jesus carried His cross and also at Calvary when she saw her son die on the cross. Other women wept as Jesus went to Calvary. He said to them, "Weep not for me but for your sins." A certain Mary washed Jesus' feet with her tears. Judas wept when he realized what he had done. Then there was Peter. He denied the Lord three times but had a chance to profess his love three times. I'm sure that there were tears in burly Peter's eye when he said to the Lord, "I love you."

We too today mourn because we are human. It is part of our human condition that we too have our losses. It's the price we pay for being human. These losses are in the hundreds. Many are small and we hardly notice them. Others are so big they take our breath away. They can destroy us if we let them. A recent article spoke of people dying of broken hearts. I've personally believed this for years.

First of all we need to admit and then name our losses. In the Book of Genesis, Adam had the chance to name the animals. Naming them was to tame them. So in the same way as we name our losses, we are able to tame them. Neu Johnson gave us a list of categories. They place the losses in four categories. It's only the fourth category that includes deaths. The categories are listed as follows:

1. Loss of possessions—i.e. pets, car keys
2. Developmental losses—i.e. retirement
3. Loss of parts of one's self—i.e. health
4. Loss of significant others—i.e. deaths, divorce

Once we've done this then the grieving process can begin. Grief is a feeling or feelings that comes with those losses. Many of us have difficulties with feelings. Just remember they exist and are part of us. In that way we have to realize that we can't ignore or deny them. See them as gifts that can be a help to us. The feelings that come with loss are anger, rage, fear, loneliness, and emptiness. These are the more violent ones and ones we are very uncomfortable with. Thus it's so easy to stifle these, which can lead to physical problems. Guilt is also a big one here. Forgiveness is a great aid here especially with realistic guilt. Unrealistic guilt simply needs to be dropped. More pleasant feelings are love, joy, happiness, contentment and also relief—relief that their suffering is over and they are at peace.

Dealing with these losses and feelings is called the mourning process. This takes time, energy, talking, tears and lots of patience with one's self. It also takes patience from others as well. We don't like this time and often want to rush it or society tells us "to get over it and move on with our life." The mourning period needs time. The Jewish community gives the mourners a year to deal with their loss or losses. This limit many times is also too soon. Today we have no time limits nor should there be time limits. We need to take the time that we need. If we take the time then it's good mourning If we cut it short then it's bad mourning. Alcohol, drugs, frivolous activity are some unhealthy responses. Walking through the pain with tears, friends and God are healthy ones. The big thing is to care for oneself as you go through your mourning time.

The book you are holding is one way of helping you during the mourning period. It began as a tribute to Dorothy Blommer, but with her guidance it has become an aid and help to anyone in mourning. Don't read it as an ordinary book. Maybe take one page at a time. Study the picture. Reflect on the words and see what feelings surface for you. Stay with it as long as you need and then write down your feelings and thoughts. See what other images come to mind, what other memories, thoughts and feelings. This may be enough for one day. You might want to share your feelings with another or simply keep them for yourself.

Enjoy the book and may it help you on your Journey of Mourning. May you find comfort.

Blessed are they who mourn,
For they will be comforted.

With Love
fr. Al

—*Fr. Al Stangl*

*L*OVE is patient, LOVE is kind. It does not
envy, it does not boast, it is not proud.
It is not rude, it is not self-seeking, it is not easily
angered, it keeps no record of wrongs.
LOVE does not delight in evil but
rejoices with the truth.
It always protects, always trusts,
always hopes, always perseveres.
LOVE NEVER FAILS.

1 Corinthians 13:4-8

Sing to the Lord with thanksgiving;
    make melody to our God on the lyre.
He covers the heavens with clouds,
    prepares rain for the earth,
    makes grass grow on the hills.

Psalm 147:7-8

My heart is steadfast, O God, my heart is steadfast;
I will sing and make melody.
Awake, my soul!
Awake, O harp and lyre!
I will awake the dawn.
I will give thanks to you, O Lord, among the peoples,
and I will sing praises to you among the nations.

Psalm 108:1-3

13

Great is our Lord, and abundant in power;
his understanding is beyond measure....
His delight is not in the strength of the horse,
nor his pleasure in the speed of a runner;
But the Lord takes pleasure in those who fear him,
in those who hope in his steadfast love.

Psalm 147:5, 10-11

14

Bless the Lord, O my soul.
O Lord my God, you are very great.
You are clothed with honor and majesty,
wrapped in light as with a garment.
You stretch out the heavens like a tent,
you set the beams of your chambers
on the waters.

Psalm 104:1-3

Before the mountains had been shaped,
 before the hills, I was brought forth—
when he had not yet made earth and fields,
 or the world's first bits of soil. . . .
Then was I beside him, like a master worker;
 and I was daily his delight.

Proverbs 8:25-26, 30

Who is God except the Lord?
And who is a rock besides our God?—
The God who girded me with strength,
and made my way safe.

Psalm 18:31-32

Sing, O heavens, for the Lord has done it;
shout, O depths of the earth;
break forth into singing, O mountains,
O forest, and every tree in it.

Isaiah 44:23

But I will sing of your might;
    I will sing aloud of your
        steadfast love in the morning.
For you have been a fortress for me
    and a refuge in the day of my distress.

Psalm 59:16

Those who live at earth's farthest bounds
are awed by your signs;
you make the gateways of the morning
and the evening
shout for joy.

Psalm 65:8

*T*he Lord will give rain for the seed with which you sow the ground, and grain, the produce of the ground, which will be rich and plenteous. On that day your cattle will graze in broad pastures.

Isaiah 30:23

21

H e split rocks open in the wilderness,
and gave them drink abundantly
as from the deep.
He made streams come out of the rock,
and caused the waters to flow down
like rivers.

Psalm 78:15-16

GRIEF, WILL IT EVER END?

How long does this painful journey take to complete? Why did this happen to me? These are questions often asked when we experience the death of a precious loved one. It is my hope that sharing my thoughts with you will help just a little to understand the "seasons," the journey of grief.

Autumn is a time of mixed experiences in nature and sometimes moves us to have mixed feelings. On the one hand, the sun is less hot but, conversely, we may not enjoy the frosty air which is a reminder that winter is coming. The leaves of autumn dance in the breeze with breathtaking, radiant colors; but, we know they will soon fall and winter will come. Autumn is rich with produce and we enjoy the sweetness of a crisp apple; but we know the ground will be barren in the months to come.

The season of Autumn holds different experiences and memories for each of us. Autumn is a time of change – a time of letting go of the beauty of our cherished flowers and trees. It is this letting go and accepting the reality of the change that hurls us into such intense feeling, that we sometimes try to deny the reality of the loss in our life, making us feel so devastated. Autumn is a time to recognize the reality, the fact of our loss: my loved one has died.

The Autumn of loss is a time of shock, numbness, disbelief, denial. Denial is a wall of protection from the raw pain that is part of a significant loss. Denial means it isn't true because I don't want it to be true. It is just too hard to believe that loss which has unraveled my life's fabric.

Autumn signifies growing recognition deep within ourselves that our loved one really has died and having our feelings catch up with our mind's comprehension. The fabric of our life has been rent and a huge piece is missing.

Winter is the season in our time of grief that leads us into and through the intensity of our pain. We try to tell a trusted friend what our heart is experiencing. We journal, we try to pray, and we cry a lot. We need family, friends, our church community, and grief groups to have safe people with whom we can share our pain. Shakespeare has said, "Give sorrow words, the grief that does not speak whispers the o'er fraught heart and bids it break." That piece of wisdom means that if we do not share the pain in our heart, we will end up living with a broken heart. Everyone goes through the winter of grief in their own way but everyone must find a healthy way to grieve. God has created us in such a way that we have feelings: they are good. Feelings tell us who we are and what is going on inside of us.

In the Winter of our grief, the seed of our grief now begins its time of gestation in the rich dark earth. It is hard to believe that in the frigid cold of the night, there is growth taking place inside of us. The fertile darkness of that unknown, a deep part of each of us, is often where our intuitive creative forces abide. God is gently walking a path of growth within us! The Christ energy enters our soul in this season in a new way.

In the Spring of our grief, we begin to acknowledge that death is part of life and that we now have a new relationship with our loved one. We find new meaning when we say in the Creed, "I believe in the communion of saints." We now have a special person who belongs to that communion of saints in heaven. That beloved person is our husband, wife, mom, dad, child, sister, brother, grandparent, grandchild, nephew, niece, friend. Yes, our loved one is still a part of our life through the communion of saints. We begin to recognize that our relationship with our loved one is now a spiritual one; that relationship still exists—but it has changed. We begin to ask the question, "Who am I now without my loved one?" Life will never be the same again and the mourning challenges us to face the fact that death can make us better – or bitter. Death changes us, too. Death has a way of helping us put life into proper perspective. We come to realize more than ever the value of our faith, family, and friends. In the Springtime of our grief, we come to know that we have learned to be more appreciative of God's gifts while we still can enjoy them. Death changes our life; it will never be the same again. But in the Springtime of grief, we learn we can live without our loved one. We come to accept a "new normal" way of life.

After all the hard work of the seasons of Autumn, Winter, and Spring, grief helps us to embrace the Summer's arrival. We begin to find relief and breathe! Some of the situations and special days of celebration may not hold such intense pain for us in the Summer of our grief. Having asked the questions, "Has this loss really happened? What does all this pain in my life really mean? Who am I now without my loved one?" We now begin to ask, "How can I go on living and loving?" We learn that it is the Christian call to go on with life and that our loved one wants us to do so without feeling guilty. We begin to reach out to others in pain with our knowing heart; we enjoy the changes in our life; we give and receive hugs that are not only because of pain and we begin to be grateful for the inner life that we find again.

To come through the numbness, the intense pain, learning to live without our loved one and going on living and loving is a long journey. To come through the seasons of grief is probably the hardest work we do in life. But with our will to live, God's grace and the love around us, we can find the life that becomes ours.

As Christians we pray the words from Ecclesiastes:

To everything there is a season, a time for every purpose under the sun: A time to be born and a time to die: a time to plant and a time to pluck up that which is planted; a time to kill and a time to heal…; a time to weep and a time to laugh; a time to mourn and a time to dance…; a time to embrace and a time to refrain from embracing; a time to lose and a time to seek…; a time to rend and a time to sew; a time to keep silent and a time to speak; a time to love and a time to hate; a time for war and a time for peace. – *Ecclesiastes 3:1-8*   —*Georganne Burr, OSB*

Then Jesus said to his disciples,
"The harvest is plentiful, but the laborers are few;
therefore ask the Lord of the harvest to send out
laborers into his harvest."

Matthew 9:37-38

Solet us not grow weary in doing what is right, for we will reap at harvest time, if we do not give up.

Galatians 6:9

For you shall go out in joy,
    and be led back in peace;
the mountains and the hills before you
    shall burst into song,
    and all the trees of the field
    shall clap their hands.

Isaiah 55:12

You show me the path of life.
In your presence there is
fullness of joy;
in your right hand are
pleasures forevermore.

Psalm 16:11

ord, you have been our dwelling place
   in all generations.
Before the mountains were brought forth,
   or ever you had formed
      the earth and the world,
   from everlasting to everlasting you are God.

Psalm 90:1-2

*A*rise, my love, my fair one,
and come away;
for now the winter is past,
the rain is over and gone.
The flowers appear on the earth;
the time of singing has come,
and the voice of the turtle dove,
is heard in our land.

Song of Solomon 2:10-12

*W*hy do you worry about clothing? Consider the lilies of the field, how they grow; they neither toil nor spin, yet I tell you, even Solomon in all his glory was not clothed like one of these.

Matthew 6:28-29

31

The wilderness and the dry land shall be glad,
the desert shall rejoice and blossom...
it shall blossom abundantly,
and rejoice with joy and singing.

Isaiah 35:1-2

As the earth brings forth its shoots,
and as a garden causes what is sown
to spring up,
so the Lord GOD will cause
righteousness and praise
to spring up before all the nations.

Isaiah 61:11

33

While God has overlooked the times
of human ignorance,
now he commands all people
everywhere to repent.

Acts 17:30

34

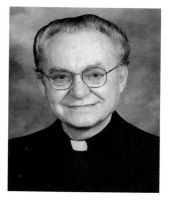

GROWING UP IN A LARGE FAMILY, then off to college and into seminary, I always lived with others in the house or a building on campus. It was the same during my first years as a priest. For about five years I was an associate with an older priest in larger parishes. Then when I was appointed administrator and pastor of my own parish, my mother came to live with me to keep house as my father had died when I was only one year old. My mother thus lived in my rectory and home for 16 years. I prayed for years that my mother's departure some day would not be sudden. I had six months' warning that my mother's days on earth were very limited. Then her funeral came on February 3, 1977. Family members remained a few more days. The next day after the last one had left, the deep grieving process began.

Now, for the first time in my life, I was living alone. That evening, of February 7, 1977, alone in a rectory, with only my office lighted, was a heart-rending experience of sorrow. As I walked by the living room, where still sat Mother's chair, and no longer was light coming from that room but I could see her chair in the faint light coming from the Marian shrine outside her window, this was breaking my heart. Mother used to say how wonderful it was to sit in that chair. She could look out and see the Shrine to Mary; she could look over at the Church where she knew Jesus was in the Most Blessed Sacrament, not far from her window. Now that chair was empty. And I was alone. Jesus and Mary sustained me.

Alone with God, sensing His indwelling in my being but sensing also a crucifixion, the burden of grieving was indeed heavy. I had assisted at funerals for years. I had gone to funeral parlors for scripture-Rosary services and conducted funeral Masses, preached on death, went to cemeteries hundreds of times for committal services. It was my duty as a priest.

In some ways I enjoyed these experiences of souls entering eternal life and the farewells of the Church I represented. And it always seemed that people were most open to the Word of God, the promise of eternal life, which I spoke at funerals. But now the grieving was mine for the one person of this world closest to me and I to her. She had left me forever, at least on this earth. How could this cross be carried. But it must be.

The thing I did not want to hear from people was: "Oh! after awhile the pain will not be so great. You will get used to it and the deep sorrow will go away." Those kind sentiments were like saying to me, "After a while you will not love your mother so much any more." And I wanted to love her deeply and always.

I placed the funeral card given to hundreds in honor of Mother's parting and with the prayer I had written behind it, onto the altar. There it remained for a very long time. I would look at it and remember my promise to Mother, "I shall remember you at the altar of God."

It was Tuesday after the funeral and I was walking down one of the sidewalks of the residential areas of Redfield, I don't know why. But I did not remain in the rectory simply feeling sorry for myself. Walking in the brisk February air I met an 80-year-old man, member of my parish. He greeted me with: "I was at your mother's funeral and I said afterwards, 'Now there is a boy who loved his mother.' It reminded me of when I lost my own mother 40 years ago."

"Do you ever get over it?" I asked the old man.

"No," he said loudly, brusquely and turned immediately and walked on without further ado.

That greeting and short remark of the old man is what I needed. Nothing and no one gave me more comfort on the natural level than that old man in his brusque reply. "Wonderful," I thought, "I shall always love my mother midst all this interior pain of separation. As I celebrated my 50th year in Christ's holy priesthood, Mother having died in my 22nd year of ordination, I still remember with gratitude that old man's comforting words.

Many flowers had been brought to the Church for my mother's funeral. There were some brown mums among them that seemed to last forever. They must have lived in their vase with water a month after the funeral. I left them in church before St. Joseph's image, as Mother had a great love for St. Joseph. Finally, I removed them.

Each night after Mother died when I would say my prayers, I would count the days that had passed since her death. Bidding farewell with my nightly prayers to another day on earth, I'd count the days, adding another day, one at a time. I'd think, for example, "This is the seventh day since Mother died." I'd keep counting each night. "It is the 25th day since Mother died." "Tonight is the 50th, 60th, 90th, 95th day since..." The night came when I said my prayers and found myself saying, "Tonight it is the 100th day since mother died."

"One hundredth?" That's enough, I thought. Mother was always a woman and mother of common sense. This is ridiculous and I must stop that counting. Mother would not want that.

No two people grieve exactly in the same way. Yes, I would have thoughts that were not always positive about the separation. But each and every time, I would then in my heart hear Mother say again one of those sentences she said to me whenever I would come to her hospital room, or as she did one day in the rectory, not long before her final illness, "I don't mind dying, but I don't want to leave you alone."

Some of Mother's words would always come to my mind to fit every grieving emotion. And they would comfort me. How did she know to say those things in the last weeks of her life, so that always there was a statement that applied to my grieving wave of emotion? How did she know? I think I know. She went through it at the age of 36 when my father left her with eight children, while I was still a baby. I remember Mother telling more than once, as my father lay dying from cancer in the Rochester, Minnesota, hospital he said to her: "You poor girl. ... You poor girl." He did not want to leave her alone so young, with eight children, most of them rather small yet.

The grieving would continue and I would remember how Mother suffered so intensely those final weeks. Finally, after about a month I thought, "I must not think of Mother simply during those final weeks of great suffering. She lived within 25 days of her 85th birthday. I must think of the many years, 49 that I knew her and they were so many tender and happy years. I must look at and remember her total life, not just the final months and especially final weeks of intense sufferings." With that thought I stopped dwelling on her physical sufferings at the end. I began to dwell on her total life. Still I wanted assurance that she was in heaven. I did not want my Mother to suffer in Purgatory.

With spring came Easter. I was engaging in all my parish activities and the growing work of the Fatima apostolate. I was writing for Catholic papers, magazines, and answering much mail that spun off from my articles, and countless phone calls. I would be conducting a youth pilgrimage in the summer of 1977 for the second time.

In the day before leaving for Fatima, Portugal, I asked our Lord, in the privacy of my own heart (without telling anyone of this prayer), that an American man whom I knew who lived in Fatima would meet me when I arrived. I asked that he then present to me a rose if my mother was in heaven. When I arrived with the youth at Fatima by bus from Lisbon, this American man, with a sack in hand, stepped up onto the bus platform. Reaching in to the sack, now about two feet higher than I stood, showered me with multi-colored rose petals. Pouring the rose petals upon me, he said, "This is for your mother."

As impressed as I was, I remembered that my prayer was for a rose, not rose petals.

One year passed and I was again back in Fatima, now to remain about six weeks as I would conduct henceforth two youth pilgrimages per summer, one for young ladies, one for young men, each 13 days in length. Directing two youth pilgrimages each summer became my practice for at least 20 years.

Knowing that I would soon leave on the two youth pilgrimages and remain in Fatima for about ten days, I prayed again to receive a sign from Our Lord and His Mother about my mother being in heaven. This time my prayer was more precise: "Dear heavenly Mother, if my mother is truly in heaven, have that American again meet me when I arrive at Fatima and this time present me, not with rose petals, but with ONE YELLOW ROSE. It must not be two roses, or a white, pink or red rose. The only sign I desire is ONE YELLOW ROSE. *Two* yellow roses will not count." That was my secret prayer.

That year, 1978, our Fatima tour-agent had problems with the airlines. It involved gathering first in Detroit, then flying to Los Angeles, consuming an entire day. Now that I was with all the 85 young ladies at the Los Angeles airport, we would leave in the evening hours for a non-stop flight from Los Angeles to Lisbon. This meant we arrived in Fatima one day late and we arrived there at midnight rather than the very early morning hours.

The nights in Fatima, Portugal, even in July and August, are usually cold so that one needs at least a jacket or sweater and a hat after sundown. When our buses pulled up to Domus Pacis in the dark of midnight, I could see this American man out in front of the building, hands in his jacket-pockets from the cold of the night. It appeared obvious to me that he held no rose.

As the bus stopped, the young people, as myself, were all somewhat exhausted from the long hours of flight. The bus-driver had opened the door for us to depart but no one stirred from our seats. We were too tired to think straight and simply sat there as if frozen. So the American entered the bus, walked down the aisle, looking from side to side, until he spotted me approximately in the middle of the bus. Standing in the aisle beside me he pulled from his pocket—ONE YEL-LOW ROSE. He presented it to me saying, "THIS IS FOR YOUR MOTHER."

Now in possession of one yellow rose as I arrived in Fatima, I became quite convinced my mother was in heaven. The man told me a few days later that he had had TWO YELLOW ROSES to present to me that morning but, when we did not arrive until midnight, during the day, he had met a person with a problem. He presented her with one of the roses, saving the other yellow rose for me.

Later, while still in Fatima, I had that one yellow rose embedded in plastic, together with a medal of St. Michael. It is said that St. Michael, together with one's Guardian Angel, and our Blessed Mother, accompany a soul to heaven. The opposite side of the medal shows the three children of Fatima kneeling before Our Lady.

That same yellow rose through the years has remained before a picture of my mother in my home. It has gone with me from parish to parish and finally, as I celebrate my 50th Anniversary in Christ's holy priesthood, it still rests before a picture of my mother in my home which is now at Hanceville, Alabama. It seems my mother and father had a part in prayers that my final years would be near the Shrine of the Most Blessed Sacrament and Monastery of Our Lady of the Angels which is associated with Mother Angelica of the Eternal Word Television Network.

The years have passed so quickly since Mother's death. And looking often at the Yellow Rose, which I see as Golden, I am reminded that my goal is heaven and to work to help others on the way.

Ever since I was first ordained, I have given my mother and my father a special blessing each evening in my prayers. I continue the practice, since. I am convinced my parents have been assisting my work in the priesthood through their prayers from heaven.

—*Fr. Robert J. Fox*

Those who eat my flesh and drink my blood have eternal life, and I will raise them up on the last day; for my flesh is true food and my blood is true drink. Those who eat my flesh and drink my blood abide in me and I in them.

John 6:54-56

Let anyone who is thirsty come to me, and let the one who believes in me drink. As the scripture has said, "Out of the believer's heart shall flow rivers of living water."

John 7:37-38

Thanks be to God, who in Christ always leads us in triumphal procession, and through us spreads in every place the fragrance that comes from knowing him.

2 Corinthians 2:14

41

If you gathered
nothing in your youth,
how can you find anything
in your old age?
How attractive is sound judgment
in the gray-haired,
and for the aged
to possess good counsel!

How attractive is
wisdom in the aged,
and understanding
and counsel in the venerable!
Rich experience
is the crown of the aged,
and their boast
is the fear of the Lord.

Sirach 25:3-6

Your steadfast love, O LORD,
extends to the heavens,
your faithfulness to the clouds.

Psalm 36:5

O come, let us sing to the LORD;
   let us make a joyful noise
      to the rock of our salvation!
Let us come into his presence
      with thanksgiving;
      let us make a joyful noise
         to him with songs of praise!
For the LORD is a great God,
      and a great King above all gods.
In his hand are the depths of the earth:
      the heights of the mountains are his also.
The sea is his, for he made it,
      and the dry land, which his hands have formed.

Psalm 95:1-5

Blessed be the name of God
from age to age,
for wisdom and power are his.
He changes times and seasons,
deposes kings and sets up kings;
he gives wisdom to the wise
and knowledge to those who
have understanding.

Daniel 2:20-21

45

Let the heavens be glad, and let the earth rejoice;
let the sea roar, and all that fills it;
let the field exult, and everything.
Then shall all the trees of the forest sing for joy
before the LORD, for he is coming,
for he is coming to judge the earth.

Psalm 96:11-13

I lift up my eyes to the hills—
from where will my help come?
My help comes from the Lord,
who made heaven and earth.

Psalm 121:1-2

The Pharisees and Sadducees came, and to test Jesus they asked him to show them a sign from heaven. He answered them, "When it is evening, you say, 'It will be fair weather, for the sky is red.' And in the morning, 'It will be stormy today, for the sky is red and threatening.' You know how to interpret the appearance of the sky, but you cannot interpret the signs of the times."

Matthew 16:1-3

"No two people experience grief in exactly the same manner. Whether male or female, old or young, Swedish or Native American, Protestant or Roman Catholic, grief is an individual process." – Elizabeth Levang

"No story of loss replicates any other." – Thomas Attig

"If it is one thing I have learned ... it's that we all grieve in our own ways and on our own schedule." –Candy Lightner

"There are no absolutes in grief. There are not reactions so universal that all, or even most, people will experience them. There is only one unalterable truth: All relationships are unique." – John James & Russell Friedman

E VERY DEATH IS DIFFERENT from every other death. None is necessarily easier for the survivor; none is necessarily more difficult, whether sudden death or protracted death. One kind does not necessarily cause more grief than the other. Each can be terribly difficult. Since no deaths are easier for the survivor, no recovery tools are necessarily more fitting, whether the grief is the result of a sudden death or a protracted one—death by suicide or death by natural causes, death of an eight-year-old or death of an eighty-year-old. It is therefore important that the griever and the caregiver must explore many options for recovery, finding something that works and then staying with it.

The longer I live, the more convinced I am that most of us just want to be understood. The bottom line in a good relationship is understanding. If a woman, for example, tells me she just doesn't love her husband any-more, it is amazing how often she is really saying: " I have never been understood. If I have a thought, the thought is wrong. If I have a feeling, I am told I should not feel that way. After years of not having my feelings legitimized, I am tired."

All of us have feelings that are almost too hard to explain. Often, these feelings are not logical. Often they have no reason to exist, but they do exist, and we want someone to understand them. People who are grieving especially need understanding. They do not want us to "fix" things for them. They do not want us to explain why things are the way they are. They do not want us to change the way they think or feel; they simply want us to understand. The opposite of understanding is not misunderstanding; it is trivializing. Often we trivialize when we try to explain away the hurts or tell them how to think. "Just Understand" is another way of saying, "Just Listen."

When bad things happen to us, we need first to establish the significance of the event. When a little boy falls down in the yard and gets a scratch on his hand, his mother cleans it off and finds there is nothing serious. But the little boy wants a bandage on it, so he can show everyone his bandaged wound, saying, "See my boo-boo." He is thus establishing the significance of the event.

People going through the death of a loved one will try to establish the significance of the loved one and the depth of the loss. Usually, we are so anxious to make them feel better that we jump in to put the best face on the loss. Instead of making the grieving person feel better, we deny them significance and trivialize the death.

"Significance" is a key to the grieving process. Those who establish significance seem to progress through the grieving process, while those who can't, seem to get stuck and make very little progress. The events we cannot establish tend to become obsessions. Often, all we need do to help someone face a loss is just let them list what they have lost and not try to make them feel better. That is the gift of understanding.

When we hurt or are in grief, it is like congestive heart failure. In heart failure our bodies are filling with fluid and we must take diuretics or we will drown. In pain, we seem to be filling up with feelings and need something to help us let the feelings out or we will drown emotionally. The diuretic for this is the listening ear of a friend. As we talk, we deal with the feelings and the pressure is lessened. We literally talk away our problems.

Sometimes friends do not listen and spend the time telling us how we should feel. We end up feeling worse. But the friend with listening ears who lets us tell our story and never offers advice nor tells us how we should feel, nor tries to put the best face on the problem helps us heal.

If we are going to help people, then we must learn how to just listen. People in pain need what Doug Manning calls the three "H's." They need us to **Hang Around, Hug Them, and Hush.** They need our presence. Nothing takes the place of being there. They need our hugs; nothing feels better than a hug when we hurt. And most of all, they need us to hush. That is the hardest one of all.

It is difficult to feel like we have done something if all we have done is listen. This leads us to say too much and sometimes we say the wrong things.

The need to say something is the reason so many people run from people in pain. They don't know what to say, so they panic and run away. That is why so many people who have lost a loved one also lose friends. That is why so many nursing home residents sit waiting for the visitors who never come. The visitors don't know what to say, so they stay away.

The sooner we learn how to be comfortable with just listening, the sooner we begin to really help people deal with the feelings that are about to drown them.

The healthiest thing we can say to someone in grief or pain is, "Feel what you feel." A person in pain cannot change how they feel, so "tell them to feel what they feel." Somehow that is a hard thing to say to a grieving person. There seems to be some force within us that just must tell people they should not feel their pain. Far too often, we try to change their feelings by trying to change their thinking. The tendency is to tell them a new way to view their problem with the hope that a new way of thinking will lead to a new way of feeling.

Unfortunately a change in thinking does not always produce a change in feelings. Feelings must be understood, accepted, and worked through before they can change. When the feelings change, the thinking will follow. It is far more important for us to accept the feelings and give the person permission to feel their pain than trying to cheer them up with some positive statement about their dilemma. If someone we love has died and we are angry at the whole world and at God, how are we supposed to feel? It makes sense we would be angry. When we let grieving people "feel what they feel," the freedom and permission begins to change those feelings and that's how healing begins to happen. When we feel what we feel, what we feel changes.

—*Diane M. Bösl, M.S., L.P., L.I.C.S.W.*
Licensed Psychologist
Licensed Independent Clinical Social Worker

Truly I tell you,
unless you change
and become
like children,
you will
never enter the
kingdom of heaven.

Matthew 18:3

*S*uch are the paths of all who forget God;
the hope of the godless shall perish.
Their confidence is gossamer
a spider's house their trust.

Job 8:13-14

52

T remble, O earth, at the presence
          of the LORD,
      at the presence of the God of Jacob,
who turns the rock into a pool of water,
      the flint into a spring of water.

Psalm 114:7-8

53

Through sloth the roof sinks in,
and through indolence the house leaks.

Proverbs 10:18

Great is the LORD, and greatly to be praised;
he is to be revered above all gods.
For all the gods of the peoples are idols,
but the LORD made the heavens.
Honor and majesty are before him;
strength and beauty are in his sanctuary.

Psalm 96:4-6

Set me as a seal upon your heart,
as a seal upon your arm;
for love is strong as death,
passion fierce as the grave.

Its flashes are flashes of fire,
a raging flame.
Many waters cannot quench love,
neither can floods drown it.

Song of Solomon 8:6-7

56

Jesus answered them: "Have faith in God. Truly I tell you, if you say to this mountain, 'Be taken up and thrown into the sea,' and if you do not doubt in your heart, but believe that what you say will come to pass, it will be done for you".

Mark 11:22-23

Happy are those who do not follow
the advice of the wicked,
or take the path that sinners tread,
or sit in the seat of scoffers;
but their delight is in the law of the
LORD,
and on his law they meditate
day and night.
They are like trees
planted by streams of water.

Psalm 1:1-3

The high mountains are for the wild goats....
O Lord, how manifold are your works!
In wisdom you have made them all;
the earth is full of creatures.

Psalm 104:18, 24

Then God said, "Let us make humankind in our image, according to our likeness; and let them have dominion over the fish of the sea, and over the birds of the air, and over the cattle, and over all the wild animals of the earth, and over every creeping thing that creeps upon the earth."

Genesis 1:26

60

*D*o not fall into the grip of passion,
or you may be torn apart as by a bull.
Your leaves will be devoured and
your fruit destroyed,
and you will be left like a withered tree.

Sirach 6:2-3

As Jesus went from there, he saw two other brothers, James son of Zebedee, and his brother John, in the boat with their father Zebedee, mending their nets, and he called them. Immediately they left the boat and their father, and followed him.

Matthew 4:21-22

My heart is steadfast, O God,
    my heart is steadfast.
I will sing and make melody.
    Awake, my soul!
Awake, O harp and lyre!
    I will awake the dawn.

Psalm 57:7-8

FOOTPRINTS

One night a man had a dream. He dreamed he was walking along the beach with the LORD. Across the sky flashed scenes from his life. For each scene, he noticed two sets of footprints in the sand; one belonging to him, and the other to the LORD.

When the last scene of his life flashed before him, he looked back at the footprints in the sand. He noticed that many times along the path of his life there was only one set of footprints. He also noticed that it happened at the very lowest and saddest times in his life.

This really bothered him and he questioned the LORD about it. "LORD, you said that once I decided to follow you, you'd walk with me all the way. But I have noticed that during the most troublesome times in my life, there is only one set of footprints. I don't understand why when I needed you the most you would leave me."

The LORD replied, "My precious, precious child, I love you and I would never leave you. During your times of trial and suffering, when you see only one set of footprints, it was then that I carried you."